LEVEL
2

Alligators and Crocodiles

Laura Marsh

NATIONAL
GEOGRAPHIC

Washington, D.C.

For Izzy and Otto —L.F.M.

Published by National Geographic Partners, LLC, Washington, D.C. 20036.

Paperback ISBN: 978-1-4263-1947-1
Reinforced Library Binding ISBN:
 978-1-4263-1948-8

Editor: Shelby Alinsky
Art Director: Amanda Larsen
Editorial: Snapdragon Books
Designer: YAY! Design
Photo Editor: Vanessa Mack
Production Assistants: Allie Allen, Sanjida Rashid

The publisher and author gratefully acknowledge the expert content review of this book by Kenneth L. Krysko, Ph.D., of the Florida Museum of Natural History, and the literacy review of this book by Mariam Jean Dreher, Professor of Reading Education at the University of Maryland, College Park.

Photo Credits

Cover, Jim Brandenburg/Minden Pictures; 1 (Chinese alligators), Jianan Yu/Reuters/Corbis; 3, Image Quest Marine/Alamy; 4–5 (UP), John Kasawa/Shutterstock; 4–5 (LO), Eric Isselee/Shutterstock; 6, Denton Rumsey/Shutterstock; 7, defpicture/Shutterstock; 9 (CTR), TJUKTJUK/Shutterstock; 9 (UP), Natali Glado/Shutterstock; 9 (LO), Steve Winter/National Geographic Creative; 10, PeterVrabel/Shutterstock; 11 (UPLE), prochasson frederic/Shutterstock; 11 (UPRT), Pete Oxford/Minden Pictures/Corbis; 11 (LO), Arco Images GmbH/Alamy; 12–13, Mike Parry/Minden Pictures; 14–15, Don Couch/Alamy; 16 (INSET), Danita Delimont/Alamy; 16–17, Mark Deeble and Victoria Stone/Getty Images; 18, Erich Schlegel/Corbis; 19, Andy Rouse/naturepl.com; 20 (UP), Becky Hale/NGS Staff; 20 (LO), Matt Propert; 21 (UP), E.O/Shutterstock; 21 (CTR LE), blickwinkel/Alamy; 21 (CTR RT), Victoria Stone & Mark Deeble/Getty Images; 21 (LO), SORBIS/Shutterstock; 22, Robert Harding World Imagery/Alamy; 23, Mike Parry/Minden Pictures; 24, Henry, P./Corbis; 25, GALLO IMAGES/Getty Images; 26, SHOWCAKE/Shutterstock; 27, Chris Johns/National Geographic Creative; 29 (CTR), Doug Perrine/naturepl.com; 29 (INSET), WILDLIFE GmbH/Alamy; 30 (UP), lluecke/iStockphoto; 30 (CTR), Joseph H. Bailey/National Geographic Creative; 30 (LO), niknikon/iStockphoto; 31 (UP), J. Gerard Sidaner/Science Source; 31 (CTR RT), Brian J. Skerry/National Geographic Creative; 31 (CTR LE), blickwinkel/Alamy; 31 (LO), clark42/iStockphoto; 32 (UPLE), WILDLIFE GmbH/Alamy; 32 (UPRT), SHOWCAKE/Shutterstock; 32 (CTR LE), Danita Delimont/Alamy; 32 (CTR RT), Natali Glado/Shutterstock; 32 (LOLE), lluecke/iStockphoto; 32 (LORT), defpicture/Shutterstock; header, dangdumrong/Shutterstock; vocabulary boxes, tapilipa/Shutterstock

National Geographic supports K–12 educators with ELA Common Core Resources.
Visit natgeoed.org/commoncore for more information.

Table of Contents

Schneider's dwarf caiman

Guess What's Different

Snap! What big teeth you have!

Crocodiles and alligators look alike. They both have huge jaws with pointed teeth. They both have a long tail. Bumpy plates cover their bodies.

Can you tell which is the alligator and which is the crocodile?

But crocodiles and alligators are different. How can you tell them apart?

Alligators have a wide snout. It is rounded and U-shaped. Alligators are usually a dark color.

Croc Talk

SNOUT: an animal's nose and mouth that stick out from its face

Alligators usually live in freshwater.

dark in color

SNOUT

Crocodiles have a thinner snout. It is pointed and V-shaped. Crocodiles are lighter in color than alligators.

Crocodiles usually live in salt water.

lighter in color

SNOUT

7

A Pile of Reptiles

Though alligators and crocodiles are different, they are both reptiles. A reptile's body has scales or bony plates.

Snakes and lizards are reptiles with scales. Alligators and crocodiles are reptiles with bony plates called scutes (scoots). Both scales and scutes help protect reptiles' bodies.

Croc Talk

REPTILE: An animal that is cold-blooded and has scaly skin. Many reptiles lay eggs on land.

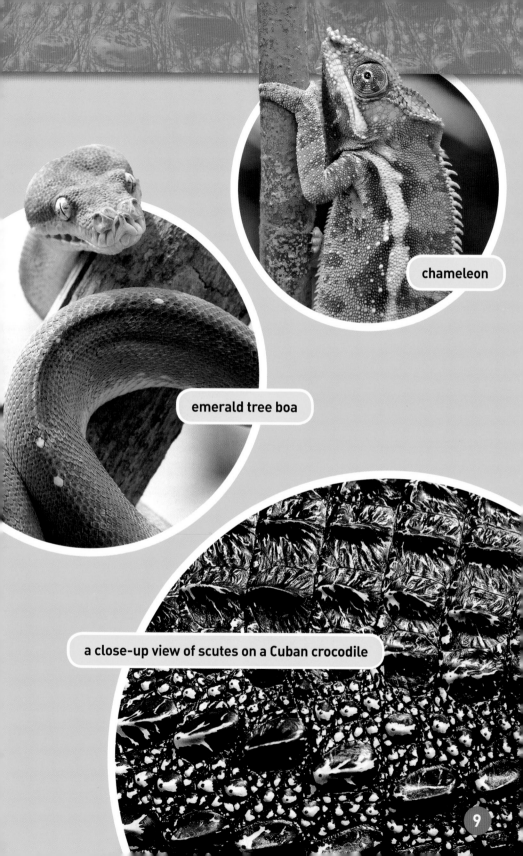

chameleon

emerald tree boa

a close-up view of scutes on a Cuban crocodile

Around the World

Alligators and crocodiles belong to a group of reptiles called crocodilians (krok-uh-DILL-ee-uns). There are 25 different kinds of crocodilians. They usually live in warm areas around the world.

Crocodilians are never far from the water. They spend a lot of time in ponds, lakes, marshes, wetlands, rivers, and swamps.

a gharial beside a lake

a broad-snouted caiman in a swamp

a slender-snouted crocodile in a river

Perfect for the Water

Alligators and crocodiles are built for living in the water. Both alligators and crocodiles have these parts.

EARS: Its ears are slits on its head. The slits close underwater.

NOSTRILS and **EYES:** Nostrils are on top of its snout. Eyes are on top of its head. A crocodilian can breathe and see while the rest of its body is underwater.

EYELIDS: Each eye has a top and a bottom eyelid. A third eyelid is clear. It protects the eye while underwater.

LUNGS: A crocodilian can hold its breath for up to two hours when its head is underwater.

TAIL: A strong tail pushes its big body through the water.

FEET: Its feet are webbed like flippers. They help a crocodilian swim quickly through the water.

BODY: It floats easily.

a young saltwater crocodile

American crocodiles

Crocodilians have excellent senses. They can see, smell, and hear better than many other reptiles. They see much better in the dark than we do.

Crocodilians have special skin, too. They can feel something moving nearby. In muddy water, they can easily find their prey.

Grabbing Dinner

Crocodilians are carnivores (CAR-nuh-vors), which means they eat meat. However, they are not picky eaters.

spectacled caiman

All kinds of fish, insects, birds, frogs, snakes, and mammals make a tasty meal. Even big animals such as antelope and buffalo are on the menu.

A Nile crocodile tries to grab a wildebeest from the herd.

American alligator

Alligators and crocodiles can go for months without eating. But when they're hungry, watch out!

A crocodilian waits for its prey to get close. Then it shoots out of the water and grabs the animal. Its big, strong jaws hold the prey underwater to drown it. Then the crocodilian gulps down dinner.

7 FUN FACTS About Crocodilians

1 Alligator teeth are hollow.

There is only one place on Earth you can find both alligators and crocodiles in the wild—southern Florida, U.S.A.

2

ALABAMA GEORGIA

ATLANTIC OCEAN

F L O R I D A

★Tallahassee

GULF OF MEXICO

Tampa

Lake Okeechobee

Approximate range of the alligator in Florida

Approximate range of the American crocodile

West Palm Beach

The Everglades

Miami

0   100 miles
0   150 kilometers

Key West

Florida Keys

3 Crocodilians lose their teeth and get new ones all through their lives.

Crocodilians grow a lot. Newly hatched young are less than a foot long. But adults are 10 to 20 feet long!

4

5

Some crocodilians lay up to 90 eggs at one time. That's a lot of babies!

Mothers come running (or swimming!) when they hear their young call for help.

6

7

Like lions, crocodilians can roar.

King of the Crocs

A saltwater crocodile feeds in a sanctuary in Australia.

The largest
crocodilian is
the saltwater
crocodile. It can
grow to more
than 20 feet long
and weigh over 2,200 pounds.
It is an excellent swimmer and
can travel far out to sea.

Saltwater crocodiles may be
the most dangerous crocodilians
of all. They are most likely to
attack—and they are deadly!

Nest and Nursery

Most reptiles lay their eggs and leave. But crocodilians stick around. They stay close to the nest and protect their young.

Some kinds of crocodilians build a mound of plants, mud, and leaves for a nest.

Other kinds of crocodilians dig a hole for a nest.

Crocodilian babies hatch from their eggs.

A mother crocodilian waits for a few months. When she hears squeaks from the eggs, she uncovers the nest. The eggs begin to hatch.

The mother gently carries the hatchlings in her mouth. She takes them to the water for their first swim. And they're off!

Croc Talk

HATCHLING: an animal that has just come out of its shell

American alligator

Endangered

New crocodilians hatch every year. But sometimes more animals die than hatch. Crocodilians can become endangered.

American alligators were once endangered. Then laws were made to protect them. Their numbers grew. Now there are over one million American alligators alive today.

Other crocodilians are now endangered. What can you do to help save these cool crocs and alligators?

The Morelet's crocodile, or Mexican crocodile, was once endangered. Now it is listed as of "least concern."

The most endangered species is the Philippine (FILL-ih-peen) crocodile. There are only about 250 left in the wild.

Croc Talk

ENDANGERED: at risk of dying out completely

QUIZ WHIZ

How much do you know about crocodilians? After reading this book, probably a lot! Take this quiz and find out.

Answers are at the bottom of page 31.

1

How many different types of crocodilians are there?

A. 4
B. 12
C. 17
D. 25

2

Alligators have a _____-shaped snout.

A. square
B. U
C. V
D. heart

Which of these is the largest?

A. the saltwater crocodile
B. the Nile crocodile
C. the American alligator
D. the Philippine crocodile

3

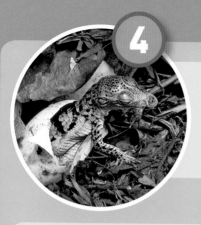

4

Baby crocodilians hatch in a _____.

A. tree
B. pond
C. nest
D. river

5

Crocodilians lose their _____ and get new ones throughout their lives.

A. teeth
B. eyes
C. ears
D. tails

6

When does a mother crocodile uncover the eggs in the nest?

A. when the moon is full
B. when she hears squeaks
C. when she's hungry
D. when it's been exactly 30 days

Crocodiles and alligators eat _____.

A. birds
B. fish
C. some big animals
D. all of the above

7

Answers: 1. D, 2. B, 3. A, 4. C, 5. A, 6. B, 7. D

ENDANGERED: at risk of dying out completely

HATCHLING: an animal that has just come out of its shell

PREY: an animal that is eaten by another animal

REPTILE: An animal that is cold-blooded and has scaly skin. Many reptiles lay eggs on land.

SENSES: sight, smell, hearing, taste, and touch

SNOUT: an animal's nose and mouth that stick out from its face